Look Out!

David Orme and Helen Bird

Contents
Warning!   2
Safety first...   3
Authentic texts   5
Glossary   16

WARNING!

After reading this book, you may be worried about all the dangers there are in the world.

DO NOT have nightmares.

Look out for
WARNING SIGNS.

Make sure you
READ WARNING SIGNS CAREFULLY

and you will be
QUITE SAFE!

Safety first...

Our world can be a dangerous place!

Storms, floods and other sorts of **severe weather** can put people in danger. In some parts of the world, **earthquake** or volcanoes can damage buildings and injure or kill people.

The world that people have made can be dangerous, too. Electrified **power lines** and other electrical equipment can kill. Roads and railway lines can be dangerous. Drivers need to be warned about dangers ahead, such as road junctions or low bridges. Railways have colour signals to tell the driver when to stop.

Some of the things we use every day can be dangerous. **Chemicals** used in kitchen or bathroom cleaners are useful but some can burn or poison people. They all need to be handled carefully.

Some metals, such as lead, can be found in everyday use and can be poisonous.

Some people work in dangerous places. They need to be warned about the risks and may have to wear special clothes.

Sometimes it is not people who need protecting. Sometimes objects in the world around us need to be protected, too. Works of art or very old objects can be damaged very easily. People need to know how to look after these things.

Some very surprising things need to be protected. Volcanoes are some of the most dangerous things in the world. But you will find out in this book that there is one volcano in America which needs protecting from people!

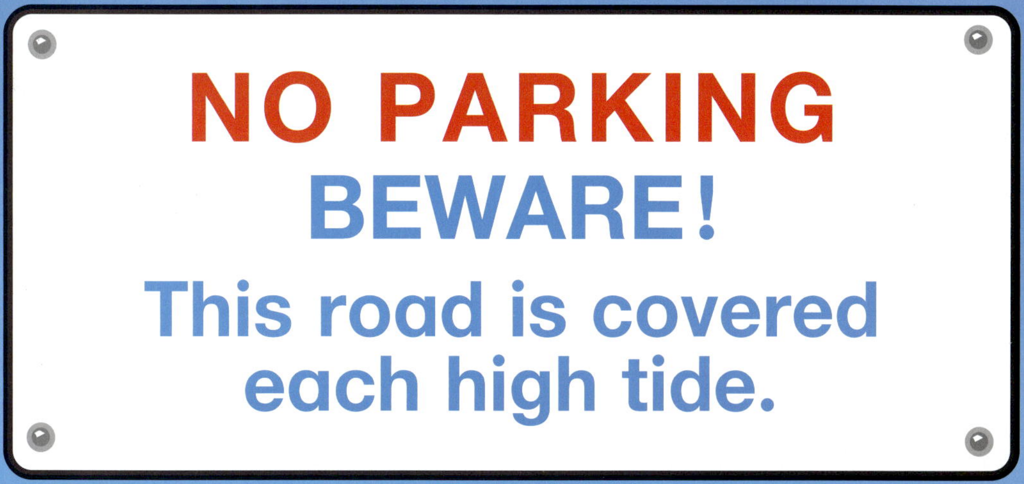
NO PARKING
BEWARE!
This road is covered each high tide.

Quayside / Riverbank

Swing bridge

Ford

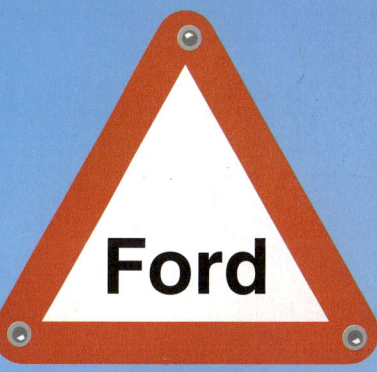

Ford

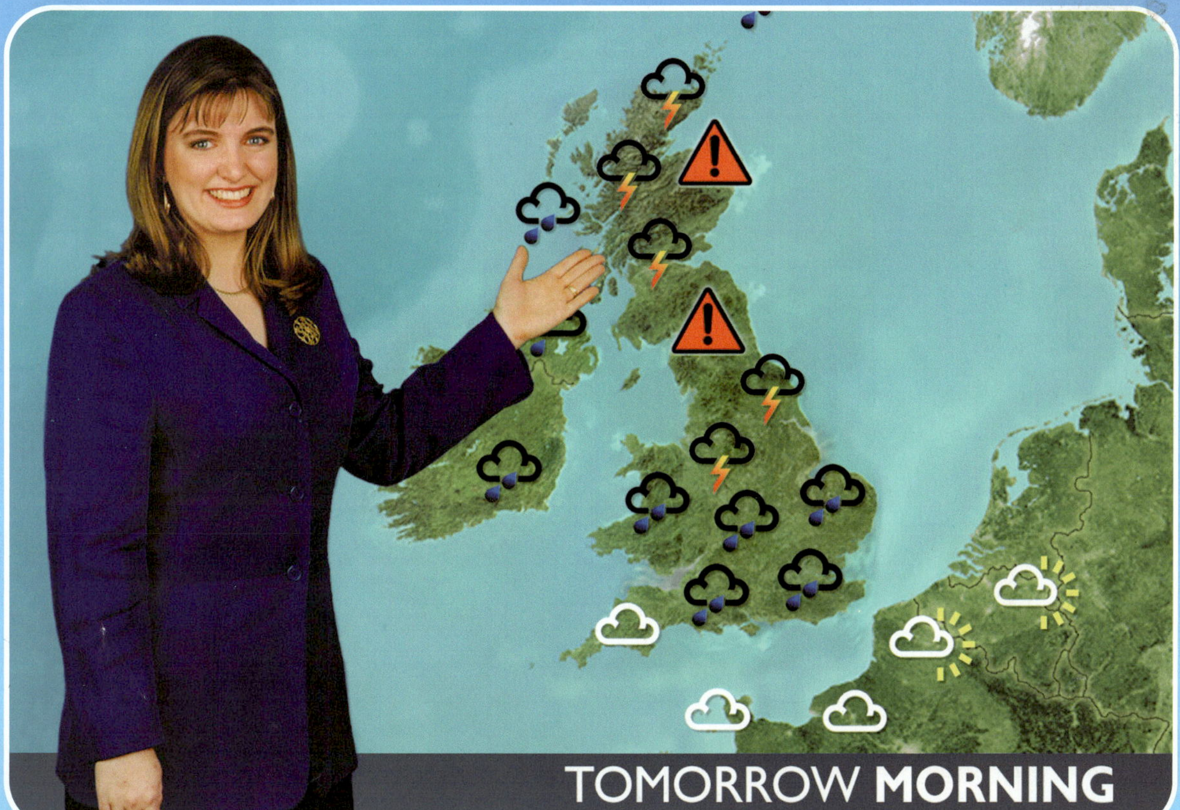
TOMORROW MORNING

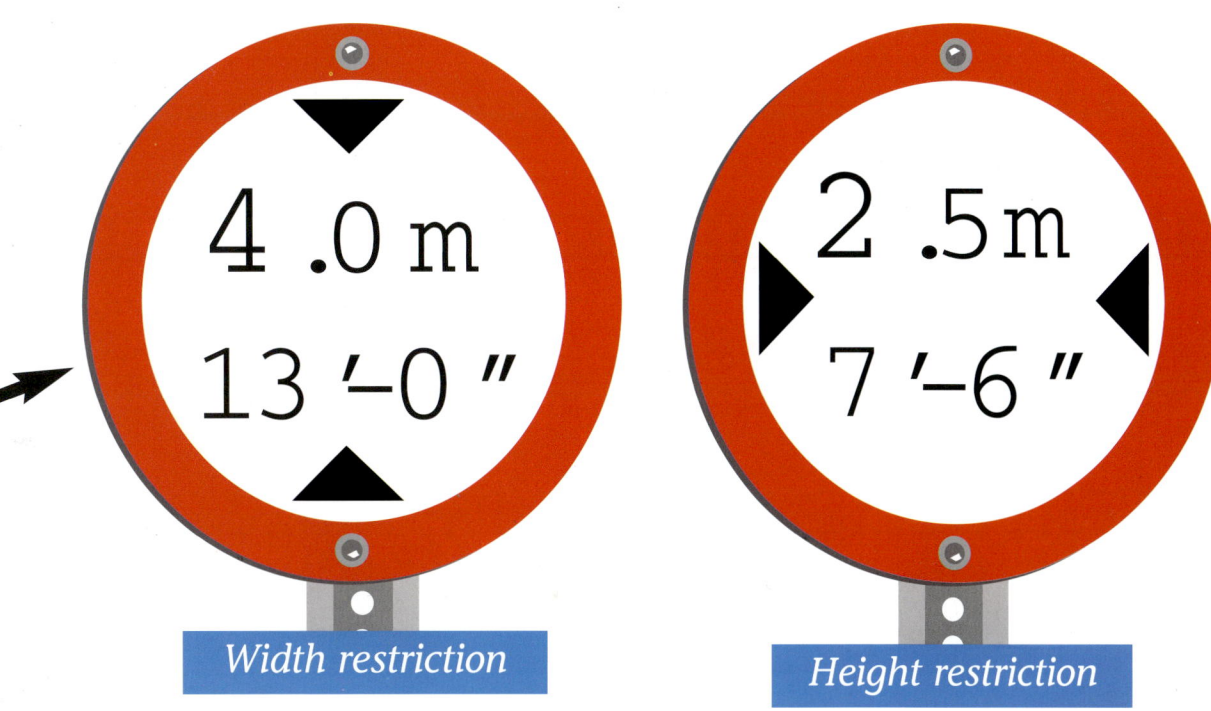

Width restriction

Height restriction

Weight restriction

⚠ Warning Web Site ⚠

| Home | Biology | Geology | Mapping | Water | Products | Glossary | Site Map | Search |

Friday, September 07, 2001, 14:02 KDT (01:02 UTC)
SHEVELUCH VOLCANO, Kamchatka
CURRENT LEVEL OF CONCERN COLOR CODE IS ORANGE

USGS Level of Concern Color Code

Green	Volcano is in its normal **"dormant"** state (normal seismicity and **fumarolic** activity is occurring).
Yellow	**Volcano is restless. Seismic activity** is elevated. Potential for eruptive activity is increased. A **plume** of gas and steam may rise several thousand feet above the volcano which may contain minor amounts of ash.
Orange	**Small ash eruption expected or confirmed. Plume(s) not likely to rise above 25,000 feet above sea level.** Seismic disturbance recorded on local seismic stations, but not recorded at more distant locations.
Red	**Large ash eruptions expected or confirmed. Plume likely to rise above 25,000 feet above sea level.** Strong seismic signal recorded on all local and commonly on more distant stations.

Mount St. Helen
Climbing Do's and Don'ts

- The Mount St. Helen's climb is not a trail hike. It is a rugged, off-trail scramble on steep terrain for people in good physical condition.

- All climbers should carry extra clothing and rain gear, sun protection for skin and eyes, extra food and water, sturdy boots, gaiters, and a first aid kit. Blowing ash can be a problem in the summer. If you plan to climb on snow, an ice axe is highly recommended.

- All climbers are required to sign in before and after their climb at the Climber's Register.

- Weather and climbing conditions can change rapidly. Wind, rain, fog, and even snow can form quickly. The temperature at the crater rim can be 20–30 degrees colder than the surrounding valleys. BE PREPARED!

- With over 13,000 registered climbers ascending the volcano each year, it is important for each climber to help minimize **human disturbance**. Stay on established routes and avoid trampling sensitive alpine plants. Use the toilets provided at Climber's Bivouac and at timberline to reduce the amount of human waste on the volcano. Pack out all litter.

Garage forecourt

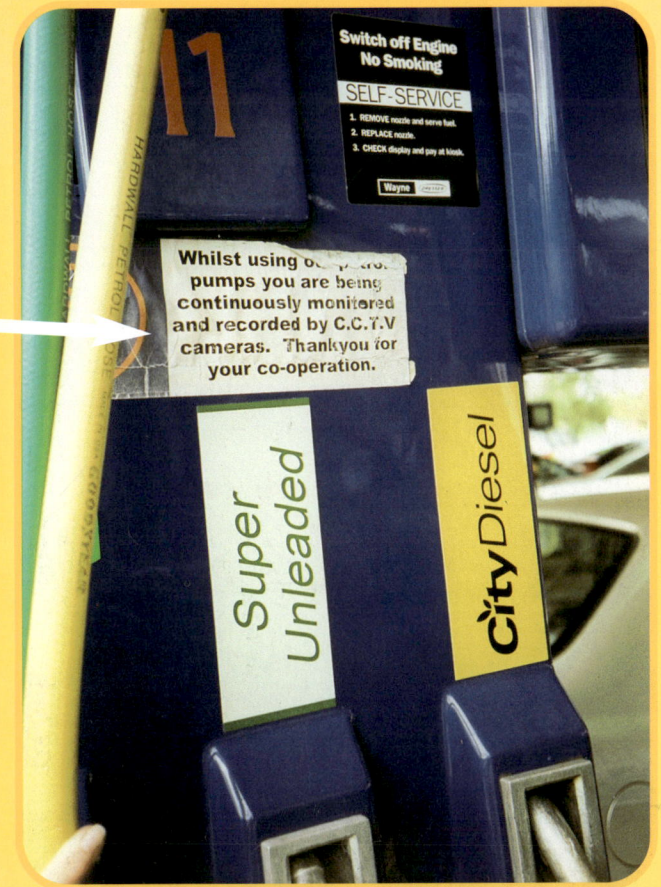

11

Radioactive

Oxdizing Agent

Spontaneous Combustible

Toxic

Corrosive

WARNING

Flash photography **prohibited.**

Light may cause damage to paintings.

Please do not touch

Fragile artefact

13

OLDCHESTER ARCHAEOLOGICAL DIG

Notice to volunteer diggers:

Excavate objects fully before removing from the ground. – <u>Do not</u> try to pull them out.

Fragile finds such as bone or pottery should be placed in a separate <u>finds</u> tray.

Metal objects can corrode quickly in the air. They should be placed in sealed plastic bags.

If you are <u>not sure</u>, report your find to the <u>supervisor</u> before lifting from the ground.

OLDCHESTER ARCHAEOLOGICAL DIG

Warning – Deep Trench

Beware of collapsing sides

OLDCHESTER ARCHAEOLOGICAL DIG

Warning

This site is hazardous. Authorized people only.
Hard hats must be worn at all times.

BIOLOGICAL HAZARD
This site may contain human remains.
Full **protective clothing** must be worn.

Glossary

archaeological describing something related to archaeology. Archaeology is the study of objects from the past.

artefact something that has been made by a person

Beware! Take care! Danger!

chemicals something made by chemistry. Chemistry is the study of how substances are made up and work together.

combustile describing something that will burn

corrosive describing something that can eat away at something else, or cause a wound like a burn

dormant not doing anything

earthquake the shaking of the ground caused by movement of rocks deep in the earth

eruption when a volcano starts to throw out hot molten lava, ash and gas

fragile easily broken or spoiled

fumarolic producing clouds of gas, ash or mud

hazard a danger to people, animals or things

high tide when the sea reaches its highest point on the shore, usually twice a day

human disturbance when people and the things they do make changes on the world around them

oxidizing agent a chemical that helps things to burn

plume a long, thin cloud stretching upwards into the sky

power lines the cables that allow electricity to flow for long distances

prohibited not allowed

protective clothing special clothing worn to prevent you from being harmed

quayside a place next to the sea or a river where boats are kept

radioactive describing a chemical that gives out small particles of itself. These particles can be very dangerous.

seismic activity anything to do with earthquakes

severe weather when the weather is hotter, colder, windier or wetter than normal

toxic something harmful, like poison